DOGS THROUGHOUT HISTORY™

The Story of the Golden Retriever

Heather Feldman

The Rosen Publishing Group's
PowerKids Press™
New York

For Mark, my husband and best friend.
And for Kelly, the Golden Retriever who brought us together.

Published in 2000 by The Rosen Publishing Group, Inc.
29 East 21st Street, New York, NY 10010

First Edition

Book design: Danielle Primiceri

Photo credits: Cover © Manuel Denner/International Stock; p. 4 © Donna Ikenberry/Animals Animals; p. 7 Courtesy of Danielle Primiceri and Heather Feldman; p. 8. © CNP/Archive Photos; p. 11 © Mimi Cotter/International Stock and Fritz Prenzel/Animals Animals; p. 12 © CORBIS/Judy Griesedieck; p. 15 © Ulrike Schanz/Animals Animals; p. 16 © Alan Fortune/Animals Animals; p. 19 Courtesy of the Canine Companions for Independence; p. 20 Courtesy of Heather Feldman.

Feldman, Heather L.
    The story of the golden retriever / by Heather Feldman.
        p.   cm.— (Dogs throughout history)
    Includes index.
    Summary: Relates the history of Golden Retrievers from the 1800s to today and describes their roles as hunting dogs, guide and rescue dogs, therapy dogs, and pets.
    ISBN 0-8239-5514-1 (lib. bdg.)
    1.Golden retriever—History—Juvenile literature. 2. Golden retriever—Juvenile literature. [1. Golden retriever. 2. Dogs.] I. Title II. Series.
SF429.G63F45 1999
636.752'7—dc21   98-55544
                                                                          CIP
                                                                          AC

Manufactured in the United States of America

Contents

The Golden Retriever Is Born

During the 1800s, in the European countries of England and Scotland, the sport of hunting **game birds** became popular. Hunters needed dogs to help them **retrieve** the birds they hunted. These dogs, called sporting dogs, retrieved **prey** on land or in water. In 1865, a sporting dog **breeder** in Scotland named Sir Dudley Majoribanks bought the only male yellow dog from a **litter** of black Wavy-Coated Retrievers. He named the dog Nous. Sir Dudley also bought a female yellow-brown Tweed Water Spaniel, whom he named Belle. Nous and Belle were **mated** and gave birth to four yellow puppies. These tiny, fluffy puppies were the Golden Retriever's earliest relatives. They shared some of the **characteristics** still seen in Golden Retrievers today.

◄ *Golden Retrievers are known for their warm hearts and friendly nature.*

All About the Golden Retriever

Golden Retrievers are one of the most popular dogs today. They are known for their beautiful golden coats, their fun-loving nature, and their **loyalty**. They are called retrievers because they are good hunters and like to carry objects in their mouths. Golden Retrievers are medium-sized dogs. Females usually weigh around 65 pounds and males weigh around 75 pounds. When Golden Retrievers jump up and cuddle in your lap, they seem to forget how heavy this feels! They are wonderful family pets and love to spend time with people. They get along well with other animals, too. Golden Retrievers have captured the hearts of people all over the world for many years.

Golden Retrievers like to play with other dogs. This Golden Retriever spends time with her friend, a German Shepherd. ▶

Golden Retrievers Come to America

Although Golden Retrievers were brought from Europe to the United States in the late 1800s, most of these dogs were not kept as house pets. Most Golden Retrievers were used to help hunters. They were first called Yellow Retrievers, but around 1920, their name was officially changed to Golden Retriever. The Golden Retriever's popularity as a pet grew quickly after 1974, when President Gerald Ford got Liberty, a young female Golden Retriever. Liberty and her puppies received a lot of attention around the country. Everyone loved their gentle nature and their striking good looks. Soon, Golden Retrievers became one of the five most popular dog **breeds** in America.

President Gerald Ford's dog Liberty helped to make Golden Retrievers one of the most popular dogs in America.

Hair of Gold

Golden Retrievers are known for their silky golden coats. Their fur can be straight or wavy, and it comes in different shades of gold. Some Golden Retrievers have light coats, which are white or pale yellow, and some have dark coats, which can be rust or brown-colored. No matter what the color is, a Golden Retriever's coat should be brushed every day to keep him looking his best. Some Golden Retrievers hunt, and their thick coats protect their bodies. If they have to go in the water, their coats dry easily. After a few good shakes, a Golden Retriever should be mostly dry.

The golden coat of the Golden Retriever comes in many different shades. ▶

Golden Retrievers as Guide Dogs

Golden Retrievers are very dependable dogs. They make excellent helpers for people because they are always eager to please. There are a few ways that Golden Retrievers help people every day. Some Golden Retrievers work as guide dogs. This means they help owners who are blind. A guide dog has to go to school to learn how to do this important job. Golden Retrievers are very smart, and they learn things quickly. As guide dogs, Golden Retrievers help their owners get around and avoid bumping into things. They have very sharp senses, and their great eyesight, hearing, and sense of smell help them keep their owners safe from harm.

A guide dog goes to the office with its owner.

Golden Retrievers as Hearing Dogs

Golden Retrievers are not only wonderful guide dogs for people who cannot see well, but they also make great hearing dogs. Hearing dogs **alert** their owners to important sounds, like bells and alarms, because their owners are deaf and have trouble hearing. These Golden Retrievers go to school to learn how to respond to sounds like a doorbell, a smoke alarm, a telephone, a baby crying, or a name being called. The hearing dog will touch his deaf owner with his paw and lead her to the sound. Sometimes the dog will lick his sleeping owner's face to wake her up. Golden Retrievers are not just wonderful hearing and seeing dogs, but they are also loyal companions.

14

Like other dogs, Golden Retrievers can hear about four times better than people.

Golden Retrievers to the Rescue

Sometimes dogs are needed to help rescue people during a **crisis** like an **earthquake** or an **avalanche**. Golden Retrievers are good at helping in a crisis because they are known to be **resilient** animals. This means they adjust well to different situations, like emergencies, and that they can act quickly. Golden Retrievers are often used to help locate people who are trapped or buried. These brave dogs use their sharp sense of smell to help find the victims. After an earthquake, a person might be trapped under **debris**. The Golden Retriever will sniff around until he locates the person. Then, the Golden Retriever will bark loudly to let the rescue workers know where the victim is. These special dogs have saved many people's lives.

Rescue dogs help save people's lives. This Golden Retriever works with a man in the deep cold snow.

A Golden Retriever Named Simba

Recently, Golden Retrievers have started to work as **therapy dogs**. Simba, a large, male Golden Retriever, works at a hospital in Brainerd, Minnesota. Simba graduated from a school called Canine Companions for Independence, or CCI. CCI teaches dogs how to help people who have certain **disabilities** from a sickness or an accident. Some of the patients in the hospital have trouble walking. Simba helps the patients feel **motivated**. He walks with them as they take each step. Sometimes, he just spends time with the patients because they love his company. Simba can also aid the hospital staff by opening and closing cabinets and by turning light switches on and off. Simba has helped a lot of people overcome challenges and feel happy.

Simba is a very smart and caring Golden Retriever. ▶

Golden Retrievers at Home

Golden Retrievers are great helpers and hard workers, but they are mostly known for being good pets. Golden Retrievers love being part of a family. As puppies, their tails start wagging and never seem to stop their whole life through! Golden Retrievers trust people and seem eager to make their owners happy. They are smart and easy to train. They are playful and fun, too. A Golden Retriever's favorite place seems to be at home with his family, where he can get lots of attention. It is not uncommon for a Golden Retriever to stick his nose under his owner's arm and, with a forceful nudge, get the attention he wants.

Golden Retrievers, like this one, are happiest at home with their family and their toys!

Hearts of Gold

Golden Retrievers have been an important part of people's lives for many years. Their willingness to help humans, in their roles as hunting dogs, guide dogs, hearing dogs, rescue dogs, and therapy dogs, makes the Golden Retriever one of the most respected and loved breeds today. People admire these dogs for their intelligence, energy, and spirit. Beauty and kindness are just two of the Golden Retriever's many special **qualities**. They are strong on the outside and gentle on the inside. For most people, looking into the big brown eyes of a Golden Retriever is all it takes to see their hearts of gold.

Web Sites:

http://www.alaska.net/~ragtym/index.html

http://www.geocities.com/Heartland/Ranch/4221

Glossary

alert (uh-LURT) To signal, warn, or make aware of something.

avalanche (A-vuh-lanch) When a lot of snow, rock, or earth falls down the side of a mountain.

breeder (BREED-ur) A person who brings male and female dogs together so they will have babies.

breeds (BREEDZ) Groups of animals that look very much alike and have the same kinds of relatives.

characteristics (KAYR-ik-tur-IS-tiks) Ways that someone or something looks or acts.

crisis (KRY-sys) A time that is very difficult.

debris (duh-BREE) Pieces of wood, stone, and other materials left after a disaster.

disabilities (dih-suh-BIH-lih-teez) Differences in people's bodies that make them unable to do certain things the same way others can.

earthquake (URTH-kwayk) When the ground shakes, caused by the sudden movement of rock far below the earth's surface.

game birds (GAYM BURDZ) Certain birds, like ducks, that are hunted for food.

litter (LIH-tur) A group of baby animals born to the same mother at the same time.

loyalty (LOY-ul-tee) When someone sticks by someone else and is faithful to him or her.

mated (MAY-tid) When a male and female body have joined in a special way. After mating, the female may have a baby grow inside her body.

motivated (MO-tih-vay-tid) Excited to do something.

prey (PRAY) An animal that is eaten by another animal for food.

qualities (KWAH-lih-teez) Ways that someone or something looks or acts.

resilient (rih-ZIHL-yint) Able to deal with problems or change.

retrieve (rih-TREEV) To bring back.

therapy dogs (THER-uh-pee DOGZ) Dogs that help people get better after a problem or accident.

23

Index

The Great Pumpkin Switch

story by **MEGAN McDONALD**

pictures by **TED LEWIN**

Orchard Books   New York

For Aunt Do
and Uncle Jim, the original
"Old Flypaper"
— M.McD.

For John Frank and
in memory of Betty Frank
and Tony Cosentino/Grandpa
— T.L.

Orchard Books, 95 Madison Avenue, New York, NY 10016

Manufactured in the United States of America.
Printed by Barton Press, Inc. Bound by Horowitz/Rae.
Book design by Mina Greenstein. The text of this book
is set in 16 point ITC Bookman Light. The illustrations
are watercolor paintings.
10 9 8 7 6 5 4 3 2

Library of Congress Cataloging-in-Publication Data
McDonald, Megan.
The great pumpkin switch / story by Megan McDonald ;
pictures by Ted Lewin.   p.   cm.
"A Richard Jackson book"—Half t.p.
Summary: An old man tells his grandchildren how he and
a friend accidentally smashed the pumpkin his sister was
growing and had to find a replacement.
ISBN 0-531-05450-0.   ISBN 0-531-08600-3 (lib. bdg.)
[1. Pumpkin—Fiction.   2. Brothers and sisters—Fiction.]
I. Lewin, Ted, ill.   II. Title.
PZ7.M478419Gr   1992   [E]—dc20   91-39660

Sit close now, and I'll tell you.

Me and Otto were racing down East Street on our bikes like we always did, shirts flapping in the wind, leaves scattering every which way.

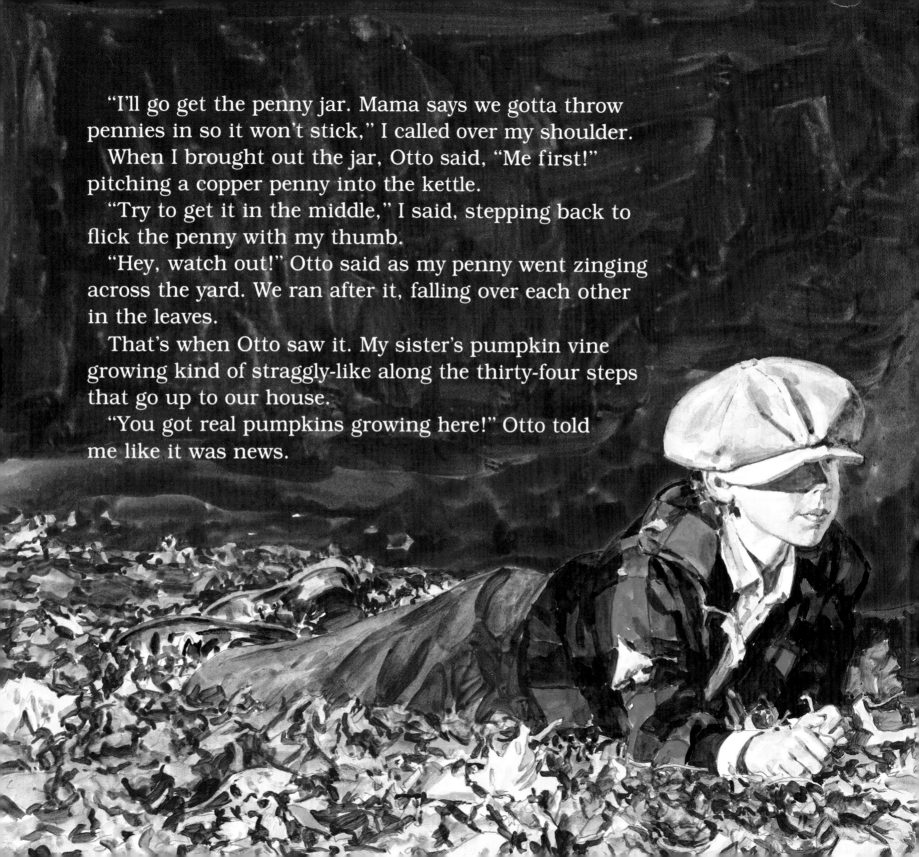

"I'll go get the penny jar. Mama says we gotta throw pennies in so it won't stick," I called over my shoulder.

When I brought out the jar, Otto said, "Me first!" pitching a copper penny into the kettle.

"Try to get it in the middle," I said, stepping back to flick the penny with my thumb.

"Hey, watch out!" Otto said as my penny went zinging across the yard. We ran after it, falling over each other in the leaves.

That's when Otto saw it. My sister's pumpkin vine growing kind of straggly-like along the thirty-four steps that go up to our house.

"You got real pumpkins growing here!" Otto told me like it was news.

We dumped our bikes in my backyard.

"Hey, Otto, it's apple butter day today. Help me stir the stuff before Mama hollers."

I lifted up the big wooden paddle. Stirred it round and round and round in that sweet-smelling soupy brown murk until our heads were spinning. Bees buzzed all around us.

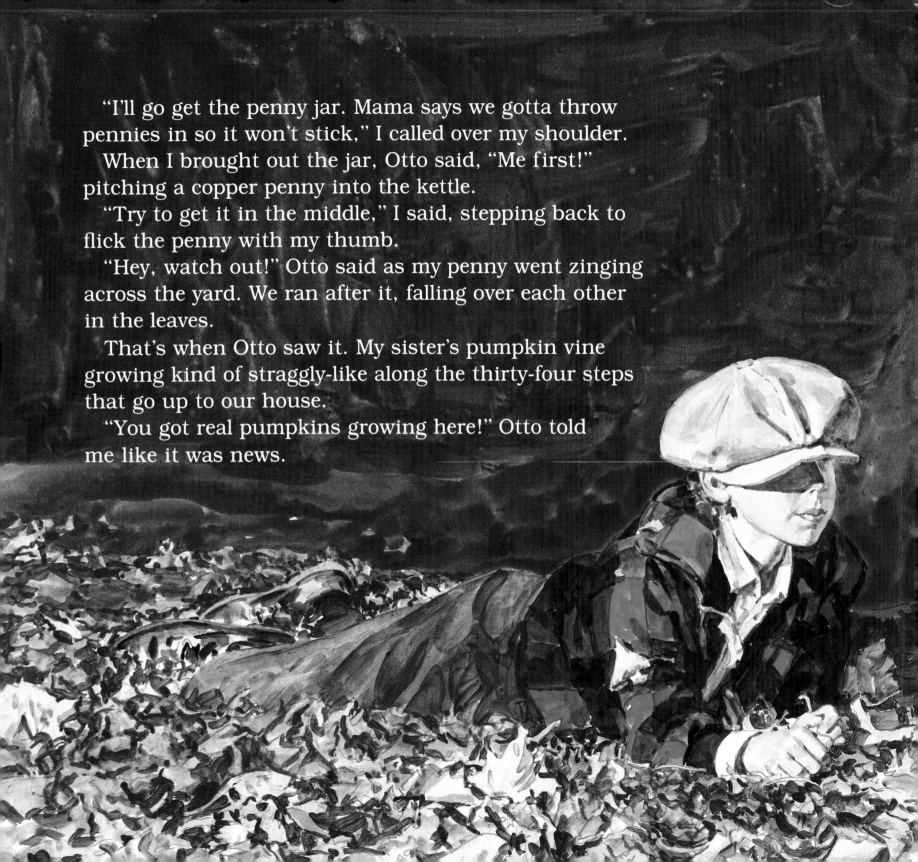

"I'll go get the penny jar. Mama says we gotta throw pennies in so it won't stick," I called over my shoulder.

When I brought out the jar, Otto said, "Me first!" pitching a copper penny into the kettle.

"Try to get it in the middle," I said, stepping back to flick the penny with my thumb.

"Hey, watch out!" Otto said as my penny went zinging across the yard. We ran after it, falling over each other in the leaves.

That's when Otto saw it. My sister's pumpkin vine growing kind of straggly-like along the thirty-four steps that go up to our house.

"You got real pumpkins growing here!" Otto told me like it was news.

"Yeah, Rosie's trying to grow the biggest pumpkin ever. Bigger than a bushel basket, she says! For the Sunflower Girls."

"The *Sunflower* Girls?" Otto scrunched his cap up like it was a bonnet.

"I know, I know."

Just then we heard the *clippety-clop* of horses' hooves on the stones. "Abba-no-potata-man!"

"Hey, it's the Potato Man. I'll race ya."

"Remember when you used to be scared of old Mr. Angelo?" Otto asked.

"Was not."

"Were too."

Rosie came running out of the house and down the steps, pigtails and ribbons flying in the air.

"Mr. Angelo! Mr. Angelo! See my pumpkin? I growed it all by myself." Rosie pointed to her prize pumpkin.

"Did ya, now? She's a beaut! Will you trade her for a bag of oranges?"

" 'Course not. I'm not tradin' Big Max for any old oranges. My brother would probably just squeeze 'em in my hair. I'm trying to get Sunflower Girls' patches for my quilt. I saw about it in a seed catalog."

"Told ya." I nudged Otto. "And your pumpkin's gonna be as big as a bushel basket, right, Rosie?"

"Bigger!" Rosie stretched her arms wide.

"That I gotta see," said Mr. Angelo. "Now I better finish my rounds, and you boys better go on inside. You too, Rosie. Storm's comin'." The Potato Man's wagon was off trotting down East Street quicker than you could say "cabbage patch."

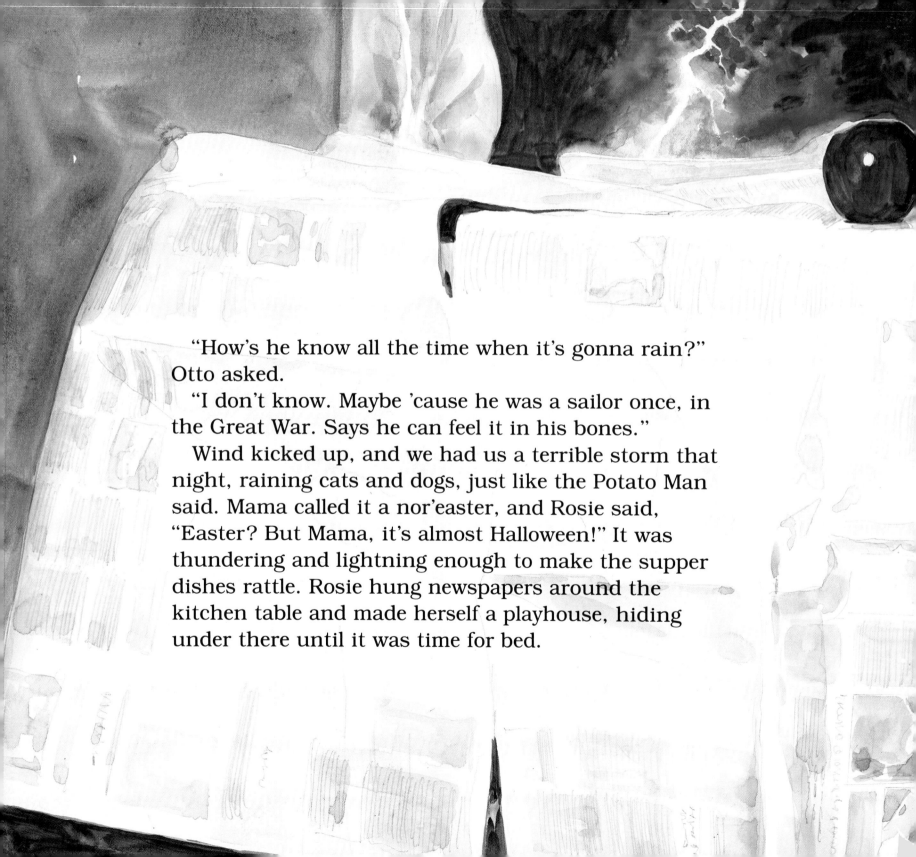

"How's he know all the time when it's gonna rain?"
Otto asked.

"I don't know. Maybe 'cause he was a sailor once, in
the Great War. Says he can feel it in his bones."

Wind kicked up, and we had us a terrible storm that
night, raining cats and dogs, just like the Potato Man
said. Mama called it a nor'easter, and Rosie said,
"Easter? But Mama, it's almost Halloween!" It was
thundering and lightning enough to make the supper
dishes rattle. Rosie hung newspapers around the
kitchen table and made herself a playhouse, hiding
under there until it was time for bed.

Middle of the night, my dog Dukie woke me up with his howling. Chocolate chip cookies were the only thing would quiet him down. Then I heard a *crrr-rrrack!* loud as Fourth of July fireworks. Mama said, "Back to bed!" but next morning our old poplar had fallen right across the front walk.

In sooner than no time, Mama had me out clearing away branches. After piano lessons, Otto came over, asked, "Why don'tcha use a saw?"

"Not allowed."

"But your mama didn't say anything about *me* not using a saw."

I ran like greased lightning around back to the toolshed, Otto right behind me, and climbed up on a barrel of soap chips to reach the saw.

Right then's when it happened.

Me and Otto were taking turns, and I was sawing away *zzz-zzzz-zzzzzhhh* when Otto yelled, "Look! Big Max!"

I looked, but I couldn't believe what I saw. Rosie's pumpkin, bouncing down the front steps, *thwump, thwump, thwump.* All thirty-four of them. Then, SPLAT!

"Pump-kin pie!" Otto laughed when he saw the squashed pumpkin at the bottom.

"Not funny, Otto. Rosie'll tell Mama, and she'll make a mashed potato out of me."

"Ah, you didn't mean to cut that vine."

"I know, but now where we gonna hide all this before Rosie sees?"

"How about Mrs. Hadley's pig next door? That pig would eat the dirty socks right off your feet."

"Here. Carry some in your shirt. Let's go!"

That pig squealed and snorted when we tossed the pieces over the fence, seeds and all.

"We could get another pumpkin before Rosie finds out, whaddya think?"

"The Potato Man!" we both said at the same time.

"Abba-no-potata-man!"

We found him down on Diploma Street. When I told him about Rosie's pumpkin, his shoulders shook laughing. "Tell you what. This here pumpkin's the biggest I got."

"It looks just like Rosie's Big Max!"

"Thing is, it'll cost you boys twenty cents."

"We got twenty cents, Mr. Angelo," I told him.

"We do?" Otto was looking at me like I just sprouted horns.

"Sure. You'll see. Can we give you the money later?"

"I think I can trust you boys until then." The Potato Man winked his good eye. "Now, let's see if you can lift this thing without making squash."

Took me and Otto both to load the Potato Man's pumpkin into my Radio Flyer wagon. "This thing must weigh fifty pounds," Otto was saying.

"Biggest pumpkin I ever did see. Hey, thanks, Mr. Angelo," I called over my shoulder.

Soon as we got home, Otto and me tied that pumpkin on the vine good as ever.

"Rosie'll never know," I told Otto.

"Hide the string under a leaf," he told me.

We barely got the saw back in the shed before Rosie came skipping down the steps. She let out a scream I'm sure they could have heard all the way down the river in Aliquippa, and went running into the house.

"She knows," I told Otto.

"You'll just have to tell her. Here she comes."

Rosie was pulling Mama's arm. "Look, Mama. Look! Look how much Big Max grew!"

"Look at that. Would you look at that," Mama was saying like she believed it. "Must have been all that rain. Right, boys?"

"Yeah, Rosie," I told her. "That rain grew your pumpkin bigger than a bushel basket."

"Big as a washtub!" Rosie laughed, spreading both arms as wide as she could reach and spinning herself in circles until she was dizzy. "Now I can get all the patches I need for my Sunflower Girls' quilt, Mama!"

"C'mon inside now, and we'll have some of that apple butter the boys worked so hard on."

"Mama, you know how all those pennies stick to the bottom?" I asked.

"Yes?"

"And you know how much you hate scrubbing out that kettle?"

"Yes!"

"If me and Otto scrub out that kettle real good, can we keep some of those pennies?"

"We'll see," Mama answered. "Right now it's time for—"

"Apple butter!"

"And hot chocolate?" Rosie asked.

Mama nodded. "And hot chocolate."

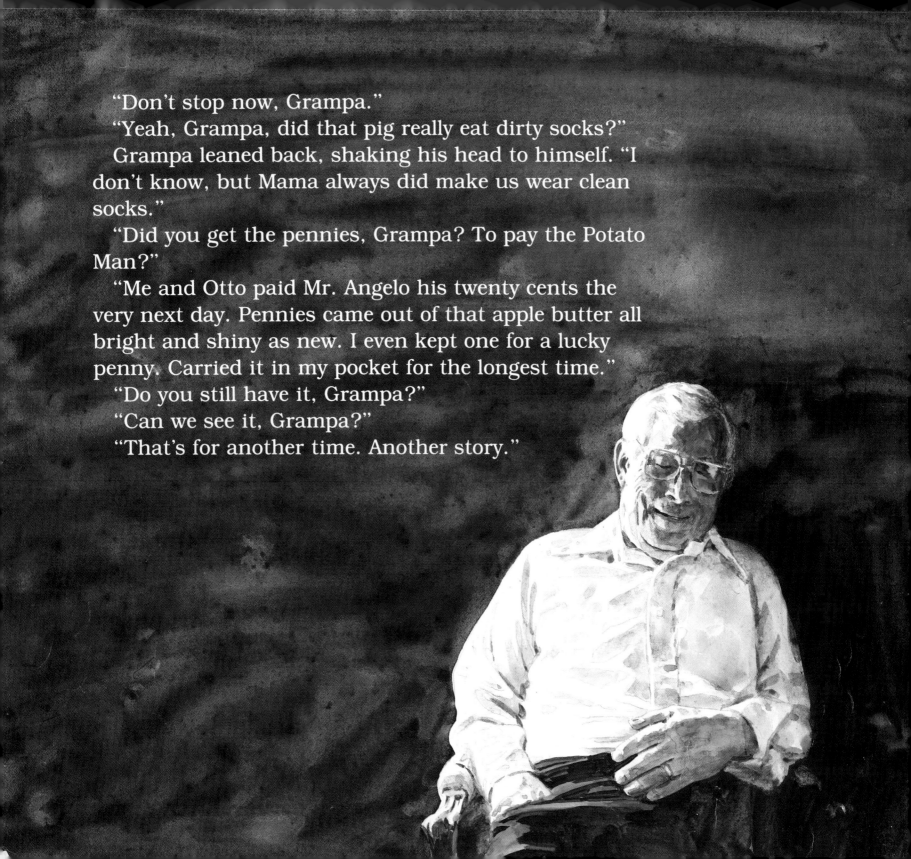

"Don't stop now, Grampa."

"Yeah, Grampa, did that pig really eat dirty socks?"

Grampa leaned back, shaking his head to himself. "I don't know, but Mama always did make us wear clean socks."

"Did you get the pennies, Grampa? To pay the Potato Man?"

"Me and Otto paid Mr. Angelo his twenty cents the very next day. Pennies came out of that apple butter all bright and shiny as new. I even kept one for a lucky penny. Carried it in my pocket for the longest time."

"Do you still have it, Grampa?"

"Can we see it, Grampa?"

"That's for another time. Another story."